For the Souls of Sisters

Speaking to the Heart, Mind, Body, Soul and Spirit of "all" Women

Dr. Mary E. Robinson

Every WOMAN is what she
lives and believes.
The JOURNEY is for the taking.

AuthorHouse™
1663 Liberty Drive
Bloomington, IN 47403
www.authorhouse.com
Phone: 1 (800) 839-8640

Published by AuthorHouse 03/12/2019

ISBN: 978-1-7283-0369-7 (sc)

Print information available on the last page.

authorHOUSE®

Contents

Acknowledgements

I thank God for inspiring me to write, live and to dream through life's journey. I thank HIM for understanding me when no one else does. Thank you for being God, even when I don't understand where you are taking me, yet I surrender to hope.

To my family, the Jackson's and the Robinson's, if there were no you, there would be no me. I love you guys. It's a joy to be a part of you. You are my roots. Jim, Baby, Booker G, and Clarissa, you are my foundation.

Sim (Daddy) and Shugg (Mommy), I love and miss you daily. C.J., Pig, and Diane, you are missed more than words can express from my heart. You're the best!

Karen Mcklerklin, your prayers for me, this book, and my life's journey has been a true friendship. Thanks for always praying so genuinely. You have always wanted to see this book published and in the lives of women.

Dedication

This book is dedicated to ALL of the beautiful women and girls of the world. You deserve the best of everything. You deserve love, respect, and life on the highest scale that can ever register. Believe and live as if the world is a billionaire waiting for you to make daily withdrawals.

No matter where you are in your journey as a woman, this book was written with you in mind. It encompasses ALL women: African-American, Caucasian, Asian, Liberian, Jamaican, Rich, or Struggling. This book is dedicated to you. I hope that you are able to find your soul, your spirit, and your experiences within the mix. More than anything, I hope that you will be encouraged to know that you are never alone on life's journey. There is no need to fly solo. As WOMEN, we are a VOICE. We are a NATION within a nation.

About the Book

"For the Souls of Sisters" is a book composed of inspirational poetic perspectives. They were written from the author's imagination and creativity. This poetry speaks to the souls, situations and experiences of "all" women, it doesn't discriminate emotionally. It reaches out and grabs the reader by the heart. It will make you nod your head, say "aww" and leave you wondering and pondering about yourself or someone you may know. It is a MUST read. Be assured that you will find this poetry quite different from most poetry that you have read. It's an instrument that probes deeply and vigorously into the soul.

The poetry is not based on anyone's real life experiences, but it is written from the perspective that women can, may have, and will possibly face some of the situations established within the content. It capitalizes on the souls, issues, and concerns that women may experience around the globe. The perspectives and ideas were written based on struggles, issues, and situations that women or anyone could possibly encounter while on life's journey.

The ultimate goal of this book is to help women of diverse backgrounds realize and understand that we as women, regardless of race, color, or creed encounter most or all of the same issues and concerns in this world we call life. Also, the goal is to give women a place to meet and creatively connect with other women who may be experiencing some of the same issues or situations, while using the opportunity to imaginatively feel that sense of compassion for another woman someone in this world who may be sitting in a corner crying, lonely, sad, or happy.

Introduction

The poetry in this book is designed to inspire and encourage women to know that life happens, and situations and experiences come in all forms. The overall objective is to let women of various backgrounds and cultures know that all women experience some of the same emotions on a day-to-day basis. My ultimate hope is that each woman who reads some or all of these poetic pieces will understand that she is never alone, and I hope that each reader will be able to take one positive take away and use it to her empowerment.

It is the hope that the poetry will create a sisterhood of women who feel and understand one another's joys, sorrows, and needs although we may never meet face-to-face due to distance, time, and travel. I also hope that this book can comfort women's minds, souls, and spirits. However, it is not recommended as a tool for psychological professional practice, unless approved legally and via the author's permission.

To all of the beautiful women and girls of the world, may we celebrate as one voice the magnificent creature that God has created us to be. He designed us purposefully. It is true that we are of different cultures. Some of us are Black, White, Indian, Arabian, Jamaican, Pakistani, and Other. Whatever the case may be, HE made us. We are here. We are alive. We can choose to live, celebrate, and appreciate the true beauty that is within our minds, hearts, souls, and spirits from day to day.

Women hurt often emotionally. In our pain, we feel the need at times to give up. We feel hopeless. We feel punished, unworthy, and helpless. Sisters, there is no need to give up on life just because someone or a situation gives up on you. There is no need to stop living and breathing because life has thrown a painful, underserved and unexpected blow. When the wind blows, dare not run. Stand with strength and force and push that pain over the cliff. Face it with a sense of hopeful expectation, believing that this can't be all and the end of all. As long as we are breathing, we deserve to live the best life possible.

Life happens. It will continue to happen. There will be good days, bad days, ups, downs, and mistakes. There will be days of power to gray skies. Whatever the case may be for you and your life, face each situation with faith, positive thinking, and unending hope. These little virtues don't cost a thing. If you live by them, you will be amazed at how rich your life will become. You will be amazed at yourself when you find the strength to laugh at your own obstacles.

As you emerge upon your journey through the pages of *For the Souls of Sisters* you will notice that the writings embark upon life's circumstances. Although the work is written in a realistic format, it does not depict the author's life or any woman's life meticulously. The poetry is written in a general format so that all women can relate. Therefore, be prepared for a self-examination and illumination of the mind, body, soul, and spirit.

May God grant all people, especially women, the strength we need to face whatever challenges enter our path. May peace be yours in all circumstances. May life grant you power, blessings, and opportunities.

Finally, my hope is that as women read the poetic pieces, they will desire to live and dream immeasurably. May you capture and recapture a desire for hope. Set high goals and expectations and achieve them all.

Let's Journey, Let's Flow, Let's Breathe-

Dr. Mary E. Robinson

Session 1:

Self-Exam 101: A Course Straight from the Heart

In Session 1, A Course Straight from the Heart, helps women to look at their life's curriculum. It presents soft pieces of a woman's internal make-up. It also looks at challenging courses that women can take on life's journey without even realizing she's writing and living the notes of her daily path, and those notes are setting her up for an end of course examination. As women we must know that we have the strength within to pass any exam with flying colors.

Girls, the journey begins here. Let's see what the curriculum holds.

Before the Mirror

If you stand before the mirror each day and can see love
and peace within your soul without any shame or guilt,
you are a woman of victor.

If you stand before the mirror each day and cannot recognize
your soul or sense of identity, something within must be
examined.

If you stand before the mirror each day and cannot see the
woman standing in your space, get to SOUL searching.
You must find that remarkable queen that is within.

If you stand before the mirror each day and feel that life is
worthless, run hurriedly in search of hope.

If you walk around day to day confused about your
existence, it is time to find your identity.

Do you know who you are? Have you found your purpose?

If you find that you are happy and at peace with the girl within,
share that light with the next struggling sister in line,
the one right next to you, standing right there, NO right there,
SHE needs you.

Help her to find her face and space in the society known as identity.

Broken Pieces

I'm feeling it. My heart is broken. My strength is gone. Here I sit amongst a thousand emotions lost and all alone.

Where must I begin describing the hurt, the pain, my confusion, the lifelessness in my entire body.

I feel like a shattered coke bottle. Once broken, it falls into many crooked parts. Most edges are jagged, rough, disfigured, out of place and glue cannot put them back together. That is my position.

Broken can have several meanings for the beholder.

How would you describe your brokenness: divorce, jobless, homeless, resentment, unfairness, childless, death of family and friends, anger toward God, self, and others, depression, bitterness, drugs, hidden secrets, guilt, the empty nester syndrome, and the list goes on and on.

Your brokenness can range from one to several things, then many. The point is, it has you TORN DOWN, BROKEN DOWN, UPSIDE DOWN, DISCOURAGED, LIFELESS, HOPELESS, SLEEPLESS, PITIFUL, MOURNING, SOUR and most of all just not living.

By now, you are ready to thrown in the tile. You tell yourself, "I am done." "I am finished." "To heck with life, you utter!" You almost despise the day you were born.

You question yourself, your identity, your birth, your list of misfortunes, and it goes on and on from dusk to dawn, dragging that long drawn out life-song.

You've cried so much until your tears are dry. They are looking back at you and questioning why. They even wonder why you allow the pain, suffering, and ongoing despair.

You tears are ready to say no more. Pick up your weapon and fight. Do not let your circumstance keep you dumped in the sewage of life. The broken pieces are beginning to smell. You deserve better.
To heal: Pull all your broken pieces together in one place. Examine each one. Lay them out before God or whomever you call your creator. Start putting them together one by one and piece by piece until you can see the image of hope, your smile, your face and place.

The mending of your broken pieces is within you. Allow the strength of your heart, your desire to heal and live, and the vision of seeing yourself on the other side of your shatteredness bring you to a place of completeness. You deserve to be a whole and not a part.

Depression

This depression is weighing me down. I feel as if I'm trapped within my thoughts and can't break free.

I don't want to be in this space that constantly stares me in the face.

Here I am, on the outside looking strong, standing tall, working my 9-5 as if I'm on top of the world, but all along my mind is twisted, confused, and spinning in ongoing circles that turns and turns out of control.

I do not like this place. I despise being in this space. My body says get up and ride, but my mind can't seem to make the stride.

This depression is controlling my mind, my soul, my body, my spirit, and yes my life.

This depression is weighing me down. I feel as if I'm trapped within my thoughts and can't break free.

I don't want to be in this space that constantly stares me in the face.

Here I am, on the outside looking strong, standing tall, working my 9-5 as if I'm on top of the world, but all along my mind is twisted, confused, and spinning in ongoing circles that turns and turns out of control.

I don't like this place. I hate being in this space. My body says get up and ride, but my mind can't seem to make the stride. This depression is controlling my mind, my soul, my body, my spirit, and yes my life.

So many situations have brought me to this den of reality. How do I rise up? How do I let go? How do I push forward, and why should I?

Wallowing in self-pity sometimes feel like a comfortable blanket. I can just lie still day after day as time slips away. There is no effort involved. Nobody bothers me, and I bother no body. All I have to do is fight with two enemies, me and the devil.

Guess what, both are winning, and I am allowing and accepting defeat. What is happening to me?

I can't continue in this downward spiral of no where to turn and no where to run.

My mind within itself is an educated weapon. It's an auditorium of tools used to rebuild and engineer my own destiny.

I was born to be a woman of strength, leadership, and encouragement to others.
God has given me education, ambition, drive, passion, and security. I am one who was born to lead, serve, and champion the world.

When I sit and let my fears conquer me, I am giving the best of my life and power away and to what and for what?

I must rise. I have to rise. I must live. I must continue to dream and present the best of me to the universe in which I exist.

So many situations have brought me to this den of reality. How do I rise up? How do I let go? How do I push forward, and why should I?

Wallowing in self-pity sometimes feel like a comfortable blanket. I can just lie still day after day as time slips away. There is no effort involved. Nobody bothers me, and I bother no body. All I have to do is fight with two enemies, me and the devil.

Guess what, both are winning, and I am allowing and accepting defeat. What is happening to me?

I can't continue in this downward spiral of no where to turn and no where to run.

My mind within itself is an educated weapon. It's an auditorium of tools used to rebuild and engineer my own destiny.

I was born to be a woman of strength, leadership, and encouragement to others.

God has given me education, ambition, drive, passion, and security. I am one who was born to lead, serve, and champion the world.

When I sit and let my fears conquer me, I am giving the best of my life and power away and to what and for what?

I must rise. I have to rise. I must live. I must continue to dream and present the best of me to the universe in which I exist.

I AM BEAUTIFUL!

Do not be afraid to say, I AM BEAUTIFUL!

If you don't know that you are beautiful say it anyway. I AM BEAUTIFUL!

Sisters, if you're overweight, it is okay to say I AM BEAUTIFUL!

If you feel that you are darker than midnight, it is okay to say, I AM BEAUTIFUL!

If you are a Caucasian sister, say it. I AM BEAUTIFUL!

If you are Hispanic, Mexican, or Ethiopian, say it. I AM BEAUTIFUL!

If you are a single mom say it extra loud and long, I AM BEAUUUUTIFUL! I AM BEYOND BEAUTIFUL. I AM BOSS!

If you are a prison mom who longs to see her children and can't because of a mistake or a misdeed, we sisters feel your pain. Somewhere inside find the courage and say it everyday, I AM BEAUTIFUL! I'll get beyond the struggle. I must continue strong.

If you are a grandma raising grandchildren that should be with the child you've raised say it, I AM BEAUTIFUL. You are a real queen.

If you are the sisters in the corners of Africa say it, I AM BEAUTIFUL!

If you are the queens of Afghanistan and the Iraqis, say it, I AM BEAUTIFUL!

To ALL little beautiful girls of the world say it, I AM BEAUTIFUL!

If you are a divorced sister, say it, I AM BEAUTIFUL! I AM WHOLE!

Sisters, you are BEAUTIFUL! You're BOLD! And You're BRAINED!

In one voice, let the all the sisters of the world SCREAM- we are BEAUTIFUL!

In one voice, let all the sisters of the world SCREAM- WE DESERVE HAPPINESS!

In one voice, let all the sisters of the world SCREAM- WE LOVE OURSELVES!

In one voice, let all the sisters of the world SCREAM- WE ARE BEAUTIFUL!

Lipstick

Lipstick can be so beautiful. It comes in many, many shades.

It brings a sense of beauty and aroma to a girl's soul, mind, body, and spirit.

It's beautiful. Wear it! We deserve all the flam and glam that a girl can achieve.

It's beautiful. If it makes you feel like Ms. America or Ms. Universe, WEAR IT!

On the side of caution, be careful to let it not become your identity or self-esteem.

Wear it. It is beautiful, just don't allow it to define you.

What happens when it rubs off? Do you still feel pretty? Do you still feel proud?

Is all the baggage from inside still screaming aloud?

Have you discovered a lipstick that can paint your soul? Search for the lipstick titled YOU.

That lipstick may be a degree, a military status, an MBA, or a new job. It doesn't matter the title, as long as it is achieving you the dreams and goals you've always wanted.

It is perfectly okay to wear lipstick from the store, just remember to fashion up any issues or concerns that's blocking your strength and ROAR.

You are the lipstick that paints your own character, your own mind, your own spirit, and your own soul.

When your lipstick shines, the whole world will wonder why it is so beautiful. They will be amazed at the spirit of beauty that it brings.

Look deep, sisters.

Put a radar on your experiences, your circumstances, and your day-to-day existence. Live like a queen with or without lipstick. You are beautiful inspite of.

Take a moment, an hour, a day, a year of for how long is needed to design a lipstick that is created with your personal touch. Make sure it is one that gives you all the beauty, shine, self-esteem and true love that your soul truly deserves.

Make it happen Queen!!!!!!!!

Deep Within

When we look into the windows of our souls, we should be able to see more than any one else can fathom. We are the only one who knows what is buried deep within.

When we look beyond the surface of doubt, fear, and disillusionment, we should be capable of conquering mountains. Our spirits should be as bold, as brave, and as calculating as that of a lion.

We should strive to become close friends with prosperity. It would be a waste of time to live life with the words "expecting to fail" written on our foreheads.

When we look within ourselves, we should be able to connect with an auditorium of internal mechanisms that pushes us beyond our weaknesses, mistakes, inabilities, and challenges.

When we look inside ourselves, we should be able to see towers of strength and skyscrapers of character that lead us beyond the doubts and limitations of others.

Where are you? Where is your mind? Where is your courage?

When we examine the inner self, we should be confident enough to know that God does not destroy dreams. He completes them. He expects us to achieve.

When we look deep within, we should be able to see the images of our history scribbled on canvas, pushing us upward versus backwards.

These images should display the beauty of motherhood, our greatness as wives, our roles as community leaders, Sunday school teachers, and sisters fighting for a cause that is invaluable to humanity.

These images should tell the story of the day we decided to take a stance against the and injustices of the world.

I hope that your personal portrait displays you as a woman of strong perception. One who is able to look beyond people's petty mistakes and focus on ideas and issues that are relevant to changing the image of a broken community.

At the end of your journey, I hope that you are able to embark upon the beauty that is inside your soul.

I hope that you are capable of realizing that you have the power to become the woman you dream about every day.

Session 2:

A Woman's Truth Will Set Her Free: Saying it Loud and Saying it Proud!

In Session 2, A Woman's Truth, is all about women putting their true situations on the line. It captures various situations that most of us girls may have encountered in life. It calls us to examine ourselves and come face-to-face with our reality. In the midst of that reality no matter what it is, we must forge ahead. We must live and not die.

I Am a Woman

I am a woman. I can use my body to turn tricks, but that's not it.
I can use my mouth to belittle others and live like that of a snitch, but that's not it.

If I choose, I could really, really be a mischievous girl. It's so easy to turn off the lights to society and create life in my own world. It takes little to no effort to build a mansion of selfishness.

I am a woman, and I choose to love. That's the best HONOR a girl can attain.

I am a woman. I am going to take every opportunity to bring out the best in my beautiful, God-given soul.

My life isn't lived according to my thighs and my eyes. I don't use my hips, and the female anatomy between my thighs to find what I think is the golden prize.

I'm just too beautiful, too wise, to settle and compromise.

I live my life as a woman because of who I am inside. I live beautifully. The unnecessary nonsense, faulty excuses, and anything else that holds me back must step aside.

Every step I take belongs to the path of my destiny. God made me to be strong, beautiful, happy, and free. I will no longer accept defeat, struggle, and misery. It's just not me.

I was never created to be a pitiful, poor, broken down soul. God has always intended for me, the woman, to live my life as someone who loves and appreciates her own soul, hair, lips, and eyes. No woman was ever meant to be a part versus a whole. The goal of life was never meant to be a broken and corrupted soul.

I am a woman. I'm not anybody's trash to be disposed. I am a spirit, a person, a soul, and a sister with a lot of class, pizzazz, originality, style and jazz.

I am so tired of telling myself that I can't. I don't have. I'm not good enough. I don't measure up, something is wrong with me. Enough of that comparison, I am just as BIG as the next man or wo---man! I am my own President and Congress.

I am tired of telling myself that I do not deserve what is best.

I am a woman. I am going to start living like the queen breathing within my soul.

I am going to take a good look at myself. I am going to take a good look at life.

I am going to look at those of whom I'm around. I'm going to take each of those entities and create a new spirit, a new goal, a new queen, a new soul.

I'm going to put on my newly found crown and truly embrace the woman, the spirit, the life, and my God-given soul.

I will no longer put me down. I am tired of such living. I'm kissing all that negativity good-bye.

Time is short. I don't know how much time I've got to live.

It would be a sad ending to have spent 20, 30, 40, 50 or 60 years of life on this earth and never felt like I have truly lived or even mattered. GIRLS, you're the BEST! OWN IT! KNOW IT!

Your soul, your spirit, and your circumstances, want let you see beyond the struggles and the bills if you keep allowing them to have control.

Take your circumstances and your bills and turn them into the real reason you were created AND THAT IS TO LIVE, TO GIVE, BE HAPPY and FULFILLED!

The question is: Do you know that you can change who you are by simply changing the way you think and the way you act? We are Women, now THAT'S AMAZING.

Big Girls

Hello Sisters-

I am a big girl. For years, I have hidden from the world.

I hid my body. I hid my face. I even hid my name. I lost my identity because I felt ashamed.

I would stand before a mirror and pray to be thin. That did not get it. I still did not realize that the issue was within.

Years and years, I tried to be Ms. Slim. I finally accepted that the dieting was just a temporary whim.

If I have tried one, I have tried them all. Diets do not work, if you are not ready for the call. My mind for change hadn't accepted the call.

I told myself time after time, it is just weight. I said, "I really don't mind." In my heart, I knew I was lying.

I finally realized that the pounds on my body were about more than just the weight.

My obesity was linked to my decision of poor dieting and stacking way too much food on my plate, along with other hidden situations.

Although it was hard, I had to admit, that I was responsible for becoming a size 36.

For days and days, I cried. I finally told myself, "No more pride." I made a decision to stand up for my life. I wanted to take control.

I didn't feel like a person. I no longer felt whole. I felt helpless with tons of holes in my soul.

I blamed my weight on the medicine. I even labeled it stress. I even said, "It was due to a lack of rest."

The excuses went far too long. Before I knew it, an extra ten pounds had grown.

In my heart and spirit, I really felt sick. I asked, "What is the trick?"

Taking charge of my life and health was not about a trick. It was about a decision to live. It was about giving me a gift of beauty that was well-deserved.

I decided that the 20-ounce cokes, potato chips, and cookies had to go. I could no longer sit back and watch my life dissolve while sneaking and eating on the down low.

My doctor told me that my life was becoming short of time, that is when the decision to lose weight became a clear and vivid picture in my mind.

My decision to lose weight was not about trying to become a size eight. It was about freedom, being happy and living to age 98.

My decision to lose weight was no longer about hiding my body, my face, and my name. It was about walking the earth without experiencing a sense of guilt, dirtiness, emptiness, and shame.

I conceptualized that my decision to lose weight is really about me. It is about the self-esteem I feel inside. It is about gaining confidence and a new sense of woman inside.

Losing weight is about loving me, being me, believing in me and owning me.

In the midst of my journey, I realized that if I am a size three or thirty-three, it is my responsibility to be the best woman that I can possibly be.

A major and important decision is to not let my weight determine who I am. I've decided to make some changes. I've decided to be happy, whether I am a size three or thirty-three and those are my final plans. I will live.

My Beautiful sisters in the struggle keep reaching for the beauty from within. It will be a matter of time before you're walking in your THIN.

Unique

Sisters, where is the love? It is okay to be unique. There is beauty in being you.

You don't have to become a different woman to embrace the society of acceptance.

You don't have to become a television image to walk as a queen. Create your own movie screen.

There are too many of us trying to become someone other than who we really are. Do we understand the meaning of loving thyself?

Are you ashamed of whom you are? Are you teaching your little girls that only thin, longhaired, light skin girls and women make superstars? NO, NO, NO!

The image has been rearranged to accompany all shades. The 21st Century has rewritten the script!

The world of opportunity is big enough to share.

It's okay to be unique. Let us raise our voices together. The First Amendment gives us the right to freedom of speech.

I love and respect my sisters of blond and brunette hair, but I love my pretty brown skin. It is what I was born to wear. It is what I was given to share, and I love my long, thick, kinky hair.

I share my uniqueness with the world from day to day- AND- I don't plan to take anything back, nor apologize for being born brown and beautiful. None of us should ever hide or subtract the beauty from which we were born. It was a GIFT!

Let's not rob each other of strength, knowledge, and opportunity.

Let's congregate to destroy the attitude of negativity and defeat.

Let's work together to create harmony, peace, love and true democracy.

If not, the wars will carry on. Separatism will continue to prolong.

Before we know it, the world will be erased, and God's most precious creation will no longer have a face of love unity, sprit and truth.

Be yourself. Embrace your uniqueness, and inspire the diversity that trod your path.

I'm Celibate and that's Okay

Ha, Ha, Ha. You are what? No way. You can't be. Don't you feel ashamed?

Sisters like you are embarrassing to the game. Don't you know that you'll get no respect? Men enjoy knowing what to expect.

If I were you, I wouldn't go around saying that too loud. Folks will think you crazy.

I'm sorry. I want to celebrate being a woman my way. I'm celebrating celibacy and it's okay.

I don't have to fall under society's expectations. There are far too many emotionally abused women due to irresponsible sexual decisions in the name of love making.

I have a choice. I am a woman. I can do as I please. I choose to remain faithful until my wedding night, if you please. Forgive me if you are offended. However, this is not an apology.

Well, I hate to tell you sister, you'll have a long wait. Once brothers know, they won't ask you for a date. Most men are not trying to wait.

Excuse me please. I believe and yet I know that are men who respect women who stay in their clothes. I don't have to get naked, jump in bed to find my night and shining armor waiting in gold.

Go on and laugh. Make me the joke of the day. I'm celibate. I'm happy and I'm okay.

Good for you if that is what you believe. Sister you don't know what you're missing-- girlfriend, please! Are you normal?

Of course I am. I don't have to contemplate herpes, HIV, and other types of disease, along with a broken heart clinging to emotional life from the bones of a terrorized soul.

The last time we conversed, you had several concerns. Come on, let's not play dumb. He left you depleted after getting some. He also despised the experience. He claimed that you were just average.

Can you say you're happy with all that is going on? Your body is continually used, and your companions move right along. You don't have one, but two, and they both make a fool out of you. Do they even know your darn name?

Hey, but like you said, that is your way. I still choose to remain celibate, and I am perfectly okay.

The time will come and it will be right. I have no problem in waiting until my wedding night.

It is sisters like you who fall prey to believe, that if you give him what he wants, he'll be pleased. Most of you are left standing alone and cold, with gunshot wounds piercing your souls.

He's left you hanging. He's moved on to the next sister who's waiting to be exposed.

It's your choice. Do as you please. I'm choosing to do it my way.

I'm celibate. I'm happy, and I am okay.

If he doesn't respect me for whom I am. That's my sign. He's not my man.

In the midst of it all, I have the final call. If I don't respect myself, neither will he. I respect my body. It will remain a mystery to be discovered and uncovered.

Go on. Do as you please. I will be here waiting to help you deal with your issues and the possibility of an unwanted disease. I'll even love you enough to not say, "I told you so."

Keep in mind, I'm not here to judge nor put you down. I'll be here like a real sister should. I'll stand and wipe your tears and coach you through the unknown, because that Mr. has departed the throne sister girl and left you ALL alone.

Sisters, it is okay to love and celebrate the beauty of your body without feeling odd or strange.

From Skills to Pills

I had it all. My name is Ms. Ph.D. I made hundreds of thousands of dollars

based upon my degree.

The big office with the glass ceiling on the 20th floor, yes I had all that and more. I was a queen of power and always the queen of the hour in my career tower.

Driving a Mesarati was my type of car. If it was not a Benz, it was the top of the line Jaguar. When I became tired of the jag, I requested a Bentley and it was what I had.

Oh no, don't make me late nor keep me waiting. Patience surely wasn't a virtue for this sister.

In my office, I called the shots. I had control of every operation. Everything was

top-notch.

Mess with me if you dare, I'd demote you and would not care.

I was one of those sisters you dare not touch. I was sharp, beautiful, and in control. Everything about me made a statement and came across quite bold.

I will admit that I had it all. There was nothing in the world I wanted and could not get.

Yes, I ranked among the fancy, the glancy, and the rich. Some would refer to me as the devil, a snake, and a witch.

My children had nannies and all. They drove them to school, karate, and baseball.

Due to having it all, I became a bit cocky. Slowly, I went for the fall.

At first, I could not see. I noticed something strange was happening to me.

I wanted something. I wanted more. What could it be? I had it all. What

was left to explore? I guess ALL in my definition just wasn't enough.

Although I was on top of the world, I did not have love. The things, the title, and

position were leading to all types of opposition, disposition, to rarely no recognition.

I began to feel lonely and miserable inside. I was not happy. My life was going wild.

I remember becoming depressed. I became fed up with making decisions and dealing with stress. I wanted freedom. I wanted peace. I wanted happiness. I just wanted to be me.

I went inside myself and screamed, "Please leave me alone." I need my space. Therefore, I unplugged the phone. I began to become unplugged.

The phone went off. The pills and other drugs came on. At the first hit I said, "Why have I waited so long?"

I began to shift from the fancy and glancy and became best friends with pills, and pills, and more pills. We were like best buds for minutes, hours, days, weeks, and months.

In my mind, my freedom started to come, but it was for the wrong price. I had no idea what was becoming the plight of my life.

Pills became my breakfast, lunch, and dinner. I thought I really had it all. I'd

become a big spender.

My life and my time became all about me. I forgot I had children and a nanny.

How could this be? My mind was totally out of reach.

In a matter of time, my hundreds of thousands of dollars were spent. You don't

have to ask where all that money went.

My life went to the dumps. I lost all I had. I became overwhelmed. I could no longer handle my position. I lost control. I no longer listened, and I lost that famous position.

I turned away the beauty that gave me my title. I took advantage of my space. I stopped caring for others. I soon fell from grace.

Power and position is never about fame. It is about humility, leadership, respect, and responsibility behind the name.

If you lose those values, you are bound to pay. Be prepared, because you will have your day.

Avoid arrogance, cockiness, and conceit. Such errors will lead to humiliation and defeat.

I went from skills to pills, but I am a determined woman. Therefore, I will continue to live.

I'll admit that I lost my place, but I am never too proud to wear an apology on my face.

If I have offended my fellowman, I ask for your forgiveness. I ask that you understand.

I'm on my journey of pulling it all back together. I'll return soon. I'll be wiser, stronger and 1000 times better.

Sisters, if this poem is you, keep striving to return and claim your strength and honor. We love you.

SNOB

Hello, it's me. You are correct. I am a S-N-O-B, and I am in love with me.

I do not understand why women around me cannot see me for the smart, up scaled individual that I am.

Yes, I like it when I have power. I like it when I am in control. I like my S-N-O-B role.

It's not my fault that you other girls come from small towns and shabby homes.

Yes, you've guessed it right. My parents were Yale and Princeton graduates. I received my first BMW at age sixteen. I enjoy being fierce and extreme.

Yes, I am bragging. I was born to be a little, rich, snobbish queen.

I know you wish you were me-- tall, beautiful, fancy, and pretty as can be. Forgive me, I am just a S-N-O-B.

Yes, I get all the guys I want. They're just a beck and call away. I can have any man I want on any given day.

Yes, I am a S-N-O-B. All of my friends are jealous of me.

Some have chosen not to come around. Hey that's okay. I won't let it get me down.

When I'm at the office, I often find myself alone. Hey that's okay. I just talk to mother on the phone. She continues to tell me that I'm her little princess.

Yes, I have it all-- fancy clothes, stylish shoes, money, make up and diamonds too.

I'm sorry it's not you. Someone has to lose.

I really don't know how to relate to women that are not of my kind. If they're not in my bracket, they are no friends of mine.

I say all of that, but I can see that my life is on the decline.

Deep within, I am lonely and in dire need of friends. I need sisters. I need love. Please forgive me for being a S-N-O-B. Please reach out to me.

I realize that all of my prestige and arrogance has found me alone. I can't continue to live on my high horse and watch the world move on.

I need your support and understanding fast. Reach out to me. My false pretenses will not last.

All of this snobbiness and entitlement is just a way of saying somebody erred along the way. I was taught to hate versus appreciate. I was taught to hate versus love.

Now, I realize that I need friends. I need love, and I need YOU. Most of all, I realize that I am no better than any other human who has been called to walk the path we call life.

Sisters, if you were taught to hate versus love, NOW is always a good time to create your difference. It is never too late to love yourself.

Simply Christian

I remember the day that I became a real Christian. I had a talk with God and knew it was time to leave the life and worldly matters that I embraced.

I ran and ran from the truth for quite awhile, but in reality, I knew I was tired of my old lifestyle. It was time to let my demons run wild. My soul was weary, tired, and restless.

When I looked into the mirror of my heart, I knew that my very existence was falling apart.

For so long, I was afraid to change. I was afraid that life wouldn't be the same. I thought my life would become a mere and boring existence, but little did I know of the power and the cheery glistening.

I remember imagining what others would think of me, but I had a choice. I could remain unhappy or be set free.

I remember opening the Bible to gain a clear understanding of what it said. Many nights, I would just sit and shake my head. I struggled with accepting God's word and what it said. It seemed to be asking more than I was willing to give.

That day to day commitment seemed to be unattainable. I just couldn't see it.

I remember tossing to and fro the decision to change or not to change. I knew that if I decided to become a Christian, it was no longer a game, and worldly pleasures wouldn't be the same.

Friends and family laughed and made jokes. Sometimes I felt embarrassed, but I knew that God had given me a sense of freedom and hope.

The cynical remarks would stab like a knife. They'd sometimes bring tears to my eyes, but I kept focused because of what I felt inside. I knew I had to relinquish my pride.

I remember friends walking away because I chose love and God as my faith. They made and poked fun. Many days I felt as if I had been on trial and jury hung. Some

days my spirit became silent and numb.

I remember all so well, one of my dearest and best friends laughed in my face. She made it clear she did not want to be in my space. The truth is, she was afraid to plead her own case. She was afraid to face the demons in her own soul.

I remember feeling weird about becoming a Christian, but I remained faithful. For the first time, I truly understood real love.

I understood what it meant to really love people of various cultures and backgrounds.

I understood that it was okay to worship God in a sanctuary with a Caucasian sister or brother, and we not look for differences in one another.

I understood that it was okay if others didn't love me because of the decision I made. This was my journey, and Jesus was there to plead my case.

Being a Christian is far beyond showing up for a Sunday morning worship service. It's a 24-hour, 365 day devotion. It's a life beyond self-centered emotions.

It doesn't mean that you have no life or lack sophistication. It's simply a new form of spiritual education. It's life on a new rotation. It's a release from your own emotional plantation.

As a Christian, I am beautiful and proud. I am an educated woman. You would be amazed at the number of people who think Christians are ignorant and have no

sense of intelligence.

I am a woman who takes a stand in the church and in public as well. Being a Christian gives me more information to support and tell. I enjoy watching the news.

It keeps me sharp and abreast of worldviews.

As a Christian, I know how to live life and have fun. I sing, I dance, and toy around with a few bands. There is nothing hypocritical in clapping my hands.

You would be amazed at how intoxicated I get from simply loving God and His word; and doing the things that matter most to me. His way of thinking is my belief system and daily philosophy, and it doesn't mean that I am weird, crazy, nor distateful.

The nightclubs are no longer my scene, but it does not mean that I am unfilled or no longer live my dreams.

I am a Christian woman, a beautiful woman, a sophisticated woman, an intelligent woman, a woman who will stand for a cause by the spirit and power of God when necessary. I will brawl for justice for all mankind, if necessary.

To all the women who are standing up for life, for righteousness, for the weak and the poor, and for the truth, I salute you for being a real woman, a Christian woman.

You have a phenomenal purpose. Therefore, be not ashamed. Take the world by storm.

Announce your freedom. Exclaim who you are. Let no one make you feel less than human, because you embrace the truth. Be amazed by the woman that lives inside of you.

Session 3:

Confused, Perplexed, So What's Next?

In Session 3, Confused, Perplexed, So What's Next, looks at how we as women sometimes get confused as to where we are in terms of our emotions, our identity, and our lives in general. This chapter also takes a peak at how we can find ourselves in situations trying to please to succeed, retain relationships while overlooking our true needs and desires. It also focuses on mistakes that women tend to make and find themselves trapped emotionally, living under the radar of unending guilt and more. Read to believe, perceive, and achieve, while making plans to walk away from your mental catastrophies.

Trapped by Secrets

What is going on? Are you being real with yourself? Are you sure you're not holding something back?

Is it true? Are you keeping a secret that you are ashamed to tell? Are you bombarded by anxiety and loaded down with guilt?

You want out. You are ready to put your secrets aside, but you are afraid to let go because of the howling inside.

Why are you afraid to talk? Why are you afraid to come face to face with the enemy who is depleting your soul?

Are you afraid that if you tell, everyone would know? Are you afraid that others may never view you the same? Are you afraid of the embarrassment that may be associated with your name?

Are you trapped by secrets while pretending to live an open and honest life? I can imagine that you have many sleepless nights. How often do you turn in your weariness?

You're trapped. What must you do? Are you ready to confess and face the truth?

It's your decision. You must do what you have to do.

People are not fools. They see that something is wrong. They may not know all the reasons as to why you do some of the things you do, but it's obvious that something deep and fierce is haunting you.

It's hard to be open and come clean, but you must talk to someone, even if it is behind the scenes. Mental health professionals were created to help us come apart at the scene.

It isn't necessary for the whole world to know your choices or mistakes. God is the only one who is perfect and lives every minute as one who is totally great.

Excuses are not encouraged. However, it may not be a bad idea to go back and reexamine the motives behind your resolutions.

Are you trapped by secrets and ready for change? Are you ready to become free and independent of whatever it is that is driving you insane?

Find a friend. Pour your heart out. Find a shoulder to lean on. Express what you're thinking and feeling. Do not be crippled by doubt.

If you can't find a shoulder to cry on, you may have to go beyond your dependence on man. Confess your situation to God. Let go and leave it in his hand.

If God is beyond your understanding and philosophy, you may have to reach out to whatever it is you believe.

In dealing with the secrecy that maybe stifling your path, remember it is not about anyone else. It is about your happiness, your freedom, and making your situations matters of the past.

It's about being able to see that you are no longer bound, but you are free at last. It is okay to leave that misery in the past. It is time to live and laugh.

Sisters, give yourself the peace and freedom that you so well deserve. That ONE situation may be the obstacle that's blocking your path to healing and understanding real love.

Used and Abused

I am tired. I am weak. I am overwhelmed. I am strained. I keep asking, "Is there anything left to gain?"

I am not sure that I can continue to live what I know isn't real. I've pretended and played the game so long.

I know within myself that I've become a living example of hypocrisy and it's wrong.

The more I live this lie, the more I continue to die.

I don't know why I haven't the courage to take a stand for what I know is right. I think it's because I fear loneliness, heartaches, and empty nights.

My mind, my soul, and my spirit are almost gone. I'm tired. I'm afraid. I'm innocent, yet stand accused. I've had enough. I don't like being abused.

I serve and serve until my strength is all gone. I never receive a thank you, but I'm the one who's always wrong.

It is pure misery and disease of the soul when you love, you give, and you're treated worse than pieces of old locked down smelly clothes that are torn beyond repair.

Do you know what it's like for someone to look you in the face and not realize you're there? The viciousness has ripped the enemy of a soul that's beyond that of someone who cares. Love for that soul seems almost impossible.

The moment I think I see a glimpse of hope, that thought becomes a frown.

I asked, "What did I do wrong?" What have I done to deserve such pain?" We both agreed to this relationship under the same name.

I am so tired of wearing a made up smile around my friends, my church, my family, my children, my neighbors, and community. Let's face it, there is no more dignity left at the residence of this soul.

I will no longer uphold and support his insecurities as a curse to my soul, my strength, and womanhood.

How long will I continue to suffer under someone else's expectation of what they think I have, when all I really have is a lie?

I've been used and abused to the point that I'm ill. I'm losing my faith, my will, and myself. Some days I'm not sure if I want to live.

No matter how much I give, it's never enough. I am so sick and tired of just dealing with stuff!

I want freedom! I want peace! I want to live! I want to know what it really means to love and be set free!

I've decided to come clean. The truth must be told. That is the only way the misery, the mistakes, the pain, and the lies will unfold.

The truth won't be pretty for a while. It will sting like that of a thousand bees, but I've got to leave the forests to see the trees. Therefore, I will start my new journey on my knees.

I know there's a message on high as my soul looks to the sky, beyond the sun and into the heart of heaven.

Used and abused, I will no longer be. I've decided to let my torturer free. It's time to live and celebrate the incredible beauty, the incredible spirit, and the incredible woman inside of me.

Sisters, if you see your life in this poem, is it speaking to you? The time for honesty may have come. What are you going to do?

It is beautiful to live and set yourself free.

Insane Voices

Hello-

Why do you look at me as if I am strange? Do you think I'm crazy? Do I look insane? Excuse my uniqueness. I'm just lost in a battle of mind games.

I'm a girl with hidden issues and scars, hiding behind my own set of prison bars. I'm searching and finding my way through my despair. I Love to breathe.

At a young age, something unexplainable happened to me. I didn't know what to think or feel. Voices started going off in my head. I didn't believe what was happening to me could be real.

I went inside my mind, searching for answers that I could not find.

When I would ask questions, the answers would not come. One day, I heard a voice. It was my imaginary friend. She began to create answers to my confusion.

She and I would talk every day. I told her that something was beginning to take my sanity away.

My friend's name is Terra. She feels my pain. She truly understands me.

At age five, the unexplainable happened again. At this point, my life spun out of control like a whirlwind.

I told Terra about that too. She said it happened to her, and she was just four.

When I bring Terra out to play, we can laugh and talk about almost anything.

I know to you my life seems strange, but if I didn't have Terra, I would not have survived the mind game. The voices make me crazy.

We are both schizoids and we know it. I have Terra and she has me. She's the other person inside my mind and space who listens and understands me. I wish that I could see her face, but she is just a mystery that brings me a sense of laughter and hope.

I am a different kind of girl, I know. My life is complicated. I don't expect you to understand the voices inside my head. They are a constant frustration.

Pray for sisters like me. It is hard to grasp normal philosophy. One minute I am sane. The next I am not. My mind and moods are always like that of a ticking clock.

Somewhere in my life, the unexplainable took me far away. I wonder if I will ever return.

Sometimes I wish I could just take the voices and send them far, far away.

I've come to believe that my peace of mind will come in Heaven. I wrote this so that you will never take your mind for granted. Mental health is a blessing, and it can be found before Heaven. You can have it now.

Thank God that you do not have to deal with insane voices. They can roam in your head from sun up to sun down, so I've been told and watched from afar.

Thank God daily for the ability to control your mind, body, and soul.

My sisters who are struggling with various types of mental illnesses, we love you. Your PEACE will come. Figure out that UNEXPLAINABLE and cast it to the desert of no return.

Abortion

Hello Mommy,

It's me. Can you hear my voice? I know you remember who I am.

I see you as you sit, think, and cry about me everyday.

I know that you had an abortion. At the time, you were filled with lots of overwhelming and painstaking emotions.

I know you feel you did what you had to do. Hold your head up. Stop allowing your decision to get the best of you.

I spoke with God this morning. He told me to tell you that you have been forgiven. He wants you to pull your life together and start living.

I want you to know that your decision may have not been right or the best in the world, BUT now, today, look at your mistake as a lesson learned.

Stop worrying. Stop crying. Give yourself a BIG, BIG hug.

If it helps your heart to feel better, I want you to know that I love you each day from Heaven.

Go on, Mommy. Please don't cry. Forgive yourself. It is time to stop asking why.

What has been done is done. Regardless of your decision, I am still your son.

I am in Heaven with the greatest Father in the world. I get to play with trucks, puppies and all. I really have it made.

There is no need to worry. The price for my life has already been paid.

Before I go, I would like to say that if you do not forgive yourself, you are going to live the rest of your life in a lonely, sad, and depressed place. I want to say, thanks for sending me to heaven. It is so beautiful here.

Before I really go, I would like to say goodnight. Here is a BIG kiss. May it last the rest of your life.

Go on, Mommy. Do not be afraid to step outside of your confused world. You have been forgiven. Go on. Run to life. Dive right in. It is worth the living.

As you run, drop your flaws one at a time. Rip off your pride. Tell your disillusionment to step aside. Drop your shame. Tell your fears no. Leave your mistakes at the back door.

Run! You have been set free. If you do not let go, you may not ever get to see me.

I love you, Mommy. I am looking forward to the day when I can touch and hold your beautiful, beautiful face.

I almost forgot. God has something else to say. This is the message He is sending your way.

He said, "He does not become angry quickly, and He has great love. He will not

scold you forever." He also said that he will not be angry forever. He stated that, "He has taken your faults as far as the east is from the west."

Psalms 103: 6-12

It is up to you to forgive yourself.

Suicide

Remember-- you were a teenager in high school. You were in love. You were head over heels.

At that time, nothing else mattered. You were in love with the man of your dreams.

You could see the wedding, the baby, and the house with the white picket fence. You were 17. No one could tell you anything. You had found the man of your dream.

One day you looked up and realized that he, the boy of your dreams, the love of your life, was lying to you, just as he was lying to the girl he is currently staring in the face.

You could not believe what you were seeing. How dare he? How could he lie to you?

He told you that you were the only one he loved, and you believed it with all of your heart. Now you feel weak, angry, and betrayed.

He didn't tell you about the baby he has on the way by another girl your age.

He never told you about the time he mentioned to his friends that you were just someone to have around. You were never special in the first place.

Once you realized that he was up to no good, you started to feel truly misunderstood. You felt like you didn't matter. You really felt like fecal deposits being flushed out to the sea.

You felt like no one loved you. You told yourself that you were ugly. You felt like the situation was your entire fault. You asked, "What did I do wrong?"

Slowly, your hope started to fade. You could not see any reason to live. Life without him would just be worthless.

Suicide, there isn't a win. You give up your freedom, your life, and your dreams, while he continues to live.

He's still chasing life, women, girls, a free smoke and a free ride. He's not concerned about you. He doesn't stop to embrace the fact that he has even hurt you.

What's sad is that he doesn't realize you no longer exist.

You are a sister who seems confused and may have lost the courage to deal with reality.

Your decision won't stop his dream. So what will your departure of this earth really mean?

Do you think he'll get the point? Or is he still hanging, laughing with the boys, possibly somewhere drunk?

Sister, suicide is not the way to go. Why give up? You'll lose in the end.

Look in the mirror. Rebuild, refocus, and redefine your own set of life guiding principles.

Have you seen the Seven Wonders of the World? Have you traveled the skies to Paris, London, and Rome? Continue to live. Come on. You've worked too hard to just throw your life away.

Don't leave! You've yet to experience true love. Do not allow your pain to rob you of your beauty, your destiny, and your world. You deserve an awesome life.

Choose to live! YOU ARE BEAUTIFUL.

Changing to Please

Often we have dreams and unlimited desires.

We long to hold and treasure the thoughts of our hearts.

Often we find ourselves pursuing approval and appeasement. Therefore, we strive to be different in order to please others. We put our true identity aside.

To be accepted, we rearrange our lives and philosophies to embrace recognition. We hope to gain a sense of self-respect in return. Many times, we get nothing.

As time moves on, we still find ourselves on a quest to measure up and meet quotas in order to feel appreciated as well as vindicated. Yet, we're left alienated.

It is a pity that we do not have enough confidence in God and ourselves to realize that our aim in life is not to run around pleading and begging for acceptance and grace from mankind, the one who is standing on borrowed time, grace, and God's authority.

We compare ourselves to the accomplishments of others and start to feel unworthy and immeasurable. The title or position we sometimes look up to is usually the most insecure and unpackaged of us all. They are often dangling from a thread of damaged emotions.

Before we know it, we are envying the plight of another and forget the capability of our own talents and strengths. Boy, do WE sell out quickly. We sell our own souls right out from under us like a piece candy being sold at the value of zero.

Allowing others to make us feel unaccomplished and unmarketable is a huge mistake and a large price to pay. Another man's position or title doesn't make him better. He or she is JUST a SERVANT with the wrong attitude and the wrong cause. They've forgotten the true meaning of loving people for who they are and where they are.

We should never let another cripple the beauty of our imagination, self-worth, image and power. You are the key and developer of your own security and intellectual tower.

Sisters, rise to the call. You are too powerful, too spirited and too wonderful to remain under the authority of control. Change because you've chosen to do so.

You are not a puppet on a string to be dangled back and forth by any master. You are the ruler of your own soul. God has given US free will. Even HE doesn't force us to please Him, so why should we let another?

Session 4:

Weak Out-of-Control -and Doing Whatever

In Session 4, Weak, Out of Control and Doing Whatever, looks at women and how we just let whatever happens, happen. We're in the moment. We're not thinking straight. We're acting weird, making irrational decisions or doing just whatever feels good for the here and now without considering the consequences. When it is all said and done, despite the emotionalism, erraticsm, and irrationalism, we still should believe that we are our number one. Despite the matter, ALWAYS walk away with your voice in your own hand.

You know you're Weak When...

You know you're weak when your momma told you not to marry that nut and you did it anyway.

You know you're weak when you meet a complete stranger and went to bed with him on the first night.

You know you're weak when you meet someone on the Internet and you turn your life savings into total debt.

You know you're weak when everything about you becomes about a man or any person.

You know you're weak when you are so fed up with your significant other and just walk away and leave everything that you have worked for in his possession.

You know you're weak when you go to work, but he stays home lying around watching soap operas, and you can't wait to get home to hear the details of what happened with Lordis and London.

You know you're weak when you allow him to take your car and you end up catching a ride to and from work.

You know you're weak when he takes your check and spends it on cigarettes and chewing tobacco and you can barely pay the bills.

You know you're weak when you refuse to listen to anybody's advice when it comes to your man. Oh no, girlfriend! He loves me. That is my Boo.

You know you're weak when you conceive a child to try and hang on to a relationship.

You know you're weak when you see he's hurting you and you say, "I know, but I love him anyway."

You know you're weak when you choose to remain in the relationship when he has nearly beaten you to death, not once, not twice, but several times.

You know you're weak when he has told you that he no longer loves you but someone else, but you continue to hang around.

You know you're weak when he keeps sticking you with the children all day. You can't go out of the house to have some time with your girlfriends, but he's always hanging with the fellows and the bros.

You know you're weak when your husband has cheated on you several times, but you keep telling yourself, I don't have enough proof, yet you're at the point of almost losing your mind, evidence is staring you in the face like the skin you wear.

You know it's true. You just don't do what you need to do.

Sisters, you know you are weak when you no longer love yourself and continue to remain in harm's way.

No circumstance or individual should ever force you to compromise your own self-worth.

Strive to love and value yourself daily. Your weaknesses can become a powerful stepping-stone to an awesome and incredible life. Use them to your advantage.

Judges 6:14 Go in the strength you have.

It doesn't matter how small or how great. You have the power to change who you are, where you live, and how you live.

Change starts within the mind.

Spent all of my Money on my Honey

You know the story. You're in love and can't see straight if straight became your first, last, and middle name.

That joker is slick. He knows he has you just where he wants you. You're spending every dime you make, not on you but for his sake.

It starts small. You're cashing that weekly check over and over, again and again, giving it all to him. You become intoxicated of cashing and giving.

From the check it goes to the 401K. You withdraw and spend and spend it all away. You don't think about the penalties on each check. You're making those loans without regret, at least not yet.

When you are down to your last penny and all that retirement, the savings, and loans are gone, he has left you empty, confused, angry and all alone. You woke up one morning and Old Boy was gone. He skedaddled.

He left without even saying good bye. He went on with another and had the audacity to look back and say to you that you don't measure up to his current girl or lover.

He told you that what you did wasn't good enough. Somehow, he no longer acknowledges your love, support, or sacrifice. He laughs and mocks your sacrifices as a joke. All of your HEART, love and genuine efforts went up in smoke. He leaves neither love nor respect in sight.

You feel abused and used like and old towel. You're hanging on to life by a thin emotional thread, finally realizing that you just didn't use your head.

By now you're feeling sick. You're feeling duped, unloved, tricked, manipulated and emotionally constipated.

The pain of being used and abused destroys the spirit for a while. It takes a minute to get back up and peel back the layers of hope. It takes a minute to get over the hurt and pain. It hurts so much to even call his name.

Guess what! Life isn't over and you will live. Pray to find strength and peace. Ask God or to whom you find solace to lead you out of this thick, long, dark corridor and back to the light of self-love, courage, peace, hope, financial security, and the power to accept and deal with the past that you can not take back.

Forgive, move forward, and let not your decision to love whom you thought was a friend hold you captive! Girl, SMILE!

I Could Not Believe

I could not believe what was happening. I really thought that Mr. Right had found me.

We met. All went well. We went from dating to fond times, to laughs, and smiles, and googly eyes and from there to wedding bells.

Soon after the bells came what felt like the fires of hell. I found myself asking, "What is this?" "What is going on?" "What went wrong?"

This can't be. We did everything right. We even relinquished consummation until the wedding night. We had the perfect set up, the perfect plan. My God, what has become of this man?

In the midst of all the beauty and the purest of relationship, brother man was deceiving, rude, and extremely slick.

The lies started and never stopped. Then, I realized that all those wedding bells and whistles were just a flop.

Sisters, I know how you feel. It's reality. Accept the fact, you got a raw deal.

Did you find yourself in the midst of a M-Y-S-T-E-R-Y that you could not explain? Some days you felt like you were absolutely crazy and insane.

After feeling insane, others made you feel the blame.

I am with you. You called the so called girlfriends you thought you could trust. They and all their gossip left you with a feeling of disgust.

They laughed and smiled in your face, but as soon as they turned their backs, they began to chat.

Life can be funny. When you are down, so-called friends are nowhere to be found.
They seem to have turned their backs and walked the opposite direction.

It is a new day. You realize that you are divorced and back to square one. How it happened may still be a puzzle.

Some days, it's good to ask God why. Why not? He sees all and hears all.

I am convinced that it was a part of life that was an unexpected experience. In the meantime, I've decided that I owe no one an explanation or words of justification.

The only words uttered will be those of consolation to another sister who has experienced the same pain.

Most of the time, our trials can seem a bit overwhelming. The trials themselves do not make us strong. It is our ability to battle the circumstances of those trials as we refuse to accept defeat, and use those life strategies that land us back on our feet.

We have to decide that life matters and make a conscious effort to live, survive, and forge ahead.

Sisters, if you've experienced divorce. Reach out to support a queen who's standing where you once stood.

Mistakes, Mess Ups, and Clean Ups

Forgive yourself. Keep on living. Keep on fighting for what is right and what you deserve.

Stop feeling less than, because you are truly more than and beyond what anyone else will ever think of you, give to you, and do for you.

You are the one to keep the jewels, diamonds, and sparkles flowing into your life.

Life is painful. At times, it's brutal, unfair, disappointing, and mean arrows are thrown at you to no fault of your own.

Keep sanitizing the unhidden blessings that we call trials. The results of every wiped stain will appear faultless with time and persistence.

Do not judge or criticize your decisions in a negative and unfruitful way. At the time, you made your decisions out of love. Your kindness will be rewarded.

Give yourself a big huge filled with lots of love and forgiveness.

Our mistakes and mess ups are thousands of miles apart, from east to west. If God doesn't hold us captive, why should we?

Psalms 103:12 - As far as the east is from the west, so far has he removed our transgressions from us.

Let there be peace and honor within.

Session 5:

Emotional Status: Up, Down, In-between, and then Some

In Session 5, Emotional Status, looks at some of the core issues of a woman's heart. It focuses on those tender matters that makes a woman feel as is she is constantly being tugged and pulled. It also focuses on some of those sweet spots in life when a girl is just living and doing her thing. Girls, no matter what, ALWAYS keep a set of beautiful roses to sniff. You are AMAZING, BEAUTIFUL, and JUST SOMEBODY.

Alone

I am a woman! So beautiful, so strong, and yet I feel empty and alone.

I know that I am smart and brave, but my hopelessness makes me misbehave. "I have to please him I always say," but in the end, I have a price to pay.

I know that I am beautiful, smart, and strong, but for some reason I feel empty and alone.

I know I need a little comfort, someone to make me feel sweet. I need someone who loves me for me, but why does he seem such a mystery?

He can't afford to buy me a cup of coffee or tea. Yet and still I say, "Oh he's so sweet." Is it because I am missing something inside of me?

The only time we talk is when I call him on the phone. Then he lies and says, "I'm just sitting here all alone." All the time I know he's telling something wrong.

I know that I am beautiful, smart, and strong, but something within me must be wrong. After all the logic, I still sit empty and alone.

Maybe he's busy today. He doesn't have time to come my way. I'll call his job. He tells the boss to say, "He is working too hard."

Girls, why do we sell ourselves short? Why do we tolerate the nonsense? Are we really that sad and alone? What happened to self-respect and courage?

What about moving on? What about building and designing our own dreams? Why can't we create our own love affair? I promise you that I am striving to become a millionaire.

Life's opportunities are just waiting out there. It's never too late to go back to school. It's never too late to fulfill some of your wildest dreams.

Are you dominated by fear and insecurity?

Life is too short. It is too precious. Time never stops. Why should we?

Sisters, if you're in the poem above know that you are not carrying the torch alone. Have you considered reexamining your definition of love. It may provide the answer as to why you feel alone. Remember this; true love always starts at home.

If you don't learn to love yourself, you will forever find yourself alone.

I Can't

I can't do it! I'm tired. I've had enough. I just can't go on!

Why Lord, why me? I've tried to live right and be the best person I could possibly be.

I've given everything. I've given my all. I've given what I don't have.

I can't. I just can't do it anymore. My soul is tired. I've got to let go.

What do you want? The battles are too tough. The struggles have gotten old.

I'm only human. Do you understand? I'm just one woman.

Sometimes I sit and wonder why I was ever born. Was I designed to be miserable, sad, and alone?

I'm so tired of looking for answers and asking why.

Therefore, I've decided to stop saying, "I can't." I've decided to get up and try.

Today is the last day that I am going to say I can't. I'm going to shout to myself "I CAN!" I will put my mind above my self-pity.

My soul, my inside, my spirit, and my mind are ready for something new and beautiful.

I will fight for my happiness. I'll use the struggles to win the battle. I will no longer sit around and let life circumstances get me down.

I will look my issues eye to eye. I'll tell them gently, "Good- bye."

This journey of defeat is over. Success has bid a large price on my mind.

My health, my life, and my happiness shall resound. I have decided to live life
like I truly mean it.

Sisters, there are times when life's temperature is boiling over. Always know that you can versus thinking that you can't. The tools are within out wit and resilience.

Their Eyes

I remember lying in recovery. I could barely wait to see my newborn baby.

My heart was excited, though my body was exhausted.

Nothing in the world could relinquish my desire to see the beauty that God allowed me to create. There had been nine months of anticipation.

I remember the day the nurse brought her cute little body in. My soul, my spirit and joy couldn't cut the grin.

My baby, my child, had immediately become my world. It was like that of a first love.

I had so many plans. We'd do cheerleading and scouting. We'd take trips. I'd watch her play with mommy's lipstick.

One day I noticed my little girl acting strange. When I'd call, she wouldn't respond to her name.

When I'd clap to get her attention, she would just stare in the distance.

I said silently, "Something isn't right." I wouldn't dare think of my child as having an abnormal plight.

As the days continued to pass by, I noticed that she couldn't say words. She'd just sit, rock, and hum. I knew right away that something wasn't learned.

I became afraid. I panicked. I began to feel on trial. My spirit started going into denial.

I said, "No not me." This ordeal couldn't be happening to my precious baby. This can't be us!

I became numb. I became afraid. I felt a sense of shame. I didn't want to have to deal with the pain.

I automatically saw frustration, devastation, and some aspects of humiliation.

Would people think that I am the cause of my child's disability? They'd say it's my fault.

The more questions pondered, the further my mind went under.

There were days when I wanted to run and hide. That was my way of dealing with my own selfish pride.

Many times, I asked God, "Why was she born?" Why was He punishing me when I did nothing wrong?"

Some days I felt like hiding her from the world. At least I wouldn't have to deal with the things that people would say and all of the unneeded stares.

You'd think my self-pity would be enough. The battle wasn't over. Eventually, I became angry with God. I said, "I denounce you, Lord!"

In my battle with God, He began to show me nothing but blessings. Each time I'd lash out, he'd whisper and say, "Do not be afraid." "I've got you and your baby in the palms of my hands."

He showed me that my child was not a curse, but an honor.

He finally told me to stop and take a look at her beautiful face. He said, "Don't be afraid to love her. Every moment will be worth the while."

I took a deep look at myself. I said, "Lord forgive me. Give me the strength I need to go beyond this test."

I love my child. Her life is my space. Each time I see her beauty and innocence, the more I understand and appreciate God's amazing grace.

Our relationship is so beautiful and strong. I enjoy watching her cheerleading, singing and moving to her own song and dance.

My little girl is a beautiful sight to me. I appreciate her being the exact image of God and me.

If you are a sister with a handicapped child, let them live. Let them beam. Their uniqueness is their life and identity. It's their beauty and handsomeness. It's their magic and their glow that deserves to shine.

They deserve hope, mercy, and grace. God chose you to love and protect them because another couldn't take your place.

I Am in Love

I finally met someone who loves me for me. I finally met someone who appreciates me. I finally met someone who really thinks that I am worth something.

I finally met someone who isn't afraid to look me in the eye.

I finally met someone who told me that it is okay to cry.

I finally met someone who is not afraid of my mistakes.

I think that I am in love. It's real love this time. I know it. I can feel it.

This time I won't be disappointed. I won't be left standing alone.

For the first time in my life, I met someone that I could really trust. The affair is not based upon lying or lust.

I am in love and I know that I am. This one is neither fake nor sham.

It feels great to know that I have someone who is absolutely crazy about me. The conversations have meaning. They run deep. Is this really real?

I finally met someone who will never cheat on me nor hurt me. The promise was made. I know that it won't be broken.

I am in love. It has finally happened for me. No one will take it away. It's too deep. It's far too strong. It will forever live on.

The relationship is special. It was designed by God in Heaven.

The love is not based on physical appearance. It's way beyond that.

It is bigger and better than any love that I have ever experienced.

Life has taught me to love me. I appreciate who I am. It doesn't matter if you don't understand.

I have learned to accept and embrace the woman that I am. I am incredible! I am me.

I have learned to love myself. I love the woman behind the mind and the mind behind the woman.

I am in love. I have learned to love, accept, respect, and appreciate me for me.

Friendship

Friendship is something precious. It is a gift that deserves much tender love and care.

Friendship entails knowing that those you love and cherish most will always be there.

Friendship goes beyond simple chats on the phone. It allows you to call your friend on what is right, although he or she may have been seriously wrong.

Friendship is about real love and honest expectations. It's about sharing the truth, despite inward hesitations.

Friendship is about laughing, loving, and keeping it real though sometimes there will be pain when truth is revealed.

Friendship is about having that someone you can tell it all to. In your expressions, you do not have to worry about the individual judging you, your views, mistakes, strengths or weaknesses.

Friendship entails mutual love and respect. It's a two way affair, where one friend builds up, love, and inspires just as much as the other.

Friendship is about the giving of you and expecting only love, respect, and honor in return versus materialistic matter.

Friendship is knowing that the relationship will come with some scars and burns and understanding that neither party is perfect. Situations will happen to test the validity of each person's love and level of commitment, and that is for REAL!

Happy Go Lucky Me

I am just one woman, and I must say that nothing ever really gets me down. I wake up each morning ready to party. I wake up from my sleep with a grin on my face.

That is just how I see life. I am going to live and be happy no matter what. If the rent doesn't get paid well, the landlord can wait. Nothing really bothers me. I am just a happy go lucky girl.

I am one of these women who live on the edge and fly by the seat of my pants everyday.

What's there to fear? As long as I can eat, sleep, and shop, I feel just fine. I am not going to let my environment bring me down.

I am just happy go lucky me. It's amazing how everything seems to go my way. It's because I don't spend time worrying from day to day. I pray, say Lord thank you and go on about my day. WHAT's GOING to be WILL BE, just like little old happy go lucky me.

Some folks say I'm crazy. I say not.

As soon as my feet hit the morning floor, I have at least 20 things I'm going to do once I exit the door.

I stop at the corner shop and get a cup of coffee to drink. It wouldn't be me not to give some guy a wink. As I am strolling to the subway to catch my bus, I know me, I am going to get into some stuff. I can't help it. I love to have fun.

No---- its not my business that the lady standing next to me is wearing red shoes with a brown dress, I have to say something to make her feel her best. In my mind I want to bury that weird looking dress.

When I reach my office, I greet the crew with a smile. I get my work done, but you better believe I have fun. I can't stand to be quiet and bored. I have to laugh. I enjoy being the life of the party.

I am sure I get on the bosses nerve. What the heck! I'm going like to spread a little office love.

I am just happy go lucky me. On my morning break, I have to do or say something crazy. Everyone in the office just say it's just that Daisy.

That's right. It's Daisy. Who are you? Are you happy? Are you excited about life? Do you live to have fun or has life circumstances left you cold and numb?

Become like happy go lucky me. Live beyond your misery. Don't be afraid to laugh. People don't really care. It's when you're quiet and strange that they began to stare, BUT who CARES about that. I'm just happy go lucky me.

Session 6:

Beginning to Make Sense

In Session 6, Beginning to Make Sense, brings women to a place of understanding, reality, acceptance, and a place of focus regarding various situations encountered. It begins to take them of the ledge to a place of observation and balance of self. The sipping of the tea is beginning to have the taste that they've been looking for throughout the book. They are beginning to embark upon a sense of calmness from some of life's calamities. For this reason, they are beginning to see clearly, walk in the beauty of nature and life with a sense of victory.

Whatever You Have Been Through

Whatever you have been through, know that it is not the end of you.

The turmoil was written to test the meaning of life that is within you.

Whatever you have been through did not leave you totally hopeless and alone. It stung your character. The purpose was to make you strong.

When going through your trials, you might have felt as if life had gotten the best of you.

How would you have known, had you given up and not held your own?

As you struggled, everything seemed weird, out of control, and strange. You probably thought your life would never be the same.

Whenever facing opposition and you seem at your worst, always think survival first.

Tell yourself, "I am going to win." Repeat those words again and again. Say them until you feel the conviction deep within.

Say to yourself, "This is not the end. I will not let my circumstances win."

Say to yourself. "I deserve more. This cannot be it. I am determined. These matters won't make me quit."

Say to yourself, "Giving up is not an option." Say it with power. "I will beat this concoction!"

Going through issues, matters, and trials of the heart may sometimes feel like a thousand bricks have landed on your soul, ripping it apart to the very core.

Experiencing problems or whatever the case maybe is never a reason to let you, the person, cease to exist.

When going through various trials, your outcome depends on your ability to confront or remain in denial.

What are you going to do?

I Finally Understand

It has taken a while, but I finally understand. I am beginning to see my life has not gone according to plan.

My life is not about people around me. It is about what I truly feel and believe deep within.

When I take a positive view on everything I see and do life happens and it happens well.

If I choose not to believe that the best can happen for me, then I have erred in my own philosophy.

I finally understand. If I want a happy and successful return, I must be that person from within.

I once heard a wise professor say, "You get from people what you give." Life's profits are based upon how you live.

Positive thoughts breed positive results. I refuse to allow negativity to become a neighbor in my soul and in my mind.

I finally understand that positive thinking is exercising faith, and faith is simply being sure of what we hope for and certain of what we cannot see.

I finally understand that if I truly believe, I am bound to achieve.

I finally understand that God did not put me on Earth to be miserable, discouraged, and alone. My success is based upon whether or not my life, my faith, and my actions are strong.

I finally understand that my happiness cannot come from anyone else. It starts with me.

I am the apprentice of my life and its outcome.

I finally understand that life is about how I choose to live or not live.

Therefore, I will set out to accomplish the desires of my heart. As long as my actions are ethical and do not hurt the plight of another, I see no need to apologize for advancing the person I am to another level.

Where Is the Plan?

If suddenly the world was snatched from under your feet, would you know how to survive?

What if the money, the fine cars, and the fancy home you placed your values in were gone? Sisters, are you prepared to pick up life and carry on?

What if your breadwinner suddenly walked away? What if God calls him home? Now it's you and the kids, and you're alone. Are you prepared to carry on?

Do you spend every dime on the latest fashion design, but your bills and bank account are lagging way behind?

Are you prepared for a rainy day? Life's circumstances come fast, unexpectantly, and can sweep you away. Don't waste resources and then start to pray.

Plan ahead. Don't assume that roses will always bloom. Life's seasons can change in the twinkling of an eye- just that fast.

Don't assume that the sun will always shine. As you work save those extra nickels and dimes.

Are you smart? Educated? Ready to take control? Plan ahead, develop strategies and set financial goals.

Do you understand the term invest? Do you understand the term save? Are you set up to win?

Are you beginning to comprehend?

Do you understand that life's circumstances aren't always fair? They will rip you to shreds and never stop to say, "I care."

Do you understand that none of us are so mighty that we cannot fall? Get a plan before you lose it all.

Child support isn't always guaranteed. It depends on the men and their nice or naughty deeds. With the judge's order, many do not take heed.

Save your pennies. Count them one by one. Pennies add up to nickels, dimes, quarters, dollars and millions. Save, invest, plan.

Feel the Rise

Wow! I can't believe it. I can see. I can feel, and I can taste the sweetness of life.

I see myself rising from the pit of despair, drain, disdain and hopelessness. I can touch and sample my dreams with the tips of my fingers. They are just that close.

My soul continues to unfold. It peeks from behind rocks and canyons of uncertainty. I feel the rise.

When I wake up each morning, I no longer dread the movement from my bed nor regret the day ahead. I feel the rise when the first pinky hit the floor.

The RISE is real. I no longer understand defeat. I feast my thoughts on greater ideas like owning a Congress seat. That is the RISE in my rotation.

I'm no longer this woman who sits around sad, lonely, depressed and stressed. I only envision what's greater and what's best.

I feel the Rise. Vision and success only sits between these two pretty eyes.

What ever I've been through, whatever I've done, I'm over the sad and lonely songs.

All I see is vision, success, and RISE between these two beautiful pretty eyes.

Sisters, as you read this poem, I hope that you put yourself in the position of the RISE!

Session 7:

Decisions and Reflections

In Session 7, Decisions and Reflections, is where we sit back and think about where we are. This is where we ask ourselves questions; engage in deep reflections as to who we are and who we are not. It is taking a deep breath and really looking at the woman that stands behind our names. It is quiz time. It is time to change and do what needs to be done in order to thrive as an amazing successful beautiful woman.

Success may come in the form of going back to school, developing a deeper relationship with God, growing closer to family and friends or taking a trip. Success may be that job promotion. Success could be as simple as finding peace, joy, love, and happiness with one's self.

Looking Within

In order to grow and change, one must identify the real person standing behind his or her name.

Does your world ever seem like a crazy place? Does it feel like everything about you is out of order or in the wrong space?

Do you really understand the person who stands behind your name? Have you truly identified the person of whom you claim?

Do you walk around from day to day feeling as if something is missing? Do you wonder why you're not developing and your spirit isn't fulfilling?

When was the last time you conversated with your soul?

If you do not take the time to search for your soul, the real you may never unfold. Life is too short to put yourself on hold.

Are you ready to look within? Be open. The first glance may cause you take a step back. You may see things that have been hidden for years, those fears, those concealed tears.

Look inside. Look at you. What do you see? I bet there's beauty on your right, love on your left, character in the center, and there's this amazing, outstanding and astonishing portrait of you. Did you know it even exist?

There is no bitterness within you. You're not the woman living in a cage with a trapped door. Anger and rage has no deposit in your existence.

What errors? What blame? What shame? You are this brilliant, magnificent queen behind your name.

Girl, it's time to walk into your future. Work to revise your story. Write your life's dissertation. Fill each line with all of your glory, honor, and beauty. Afterwards, walk that stage and earn your PhD in the "Effects of Self-Love, Self-Care and Personal Empowerment on a Woman's Soul.

Sisters, walk into your existence.

This Is What I Have Decided

I have decided that it is great to be a woman. Because I am a woman, I know that I and all women must see the importance in understanding and loving ourselves at all times. We do not need permission to practice the art of self-appreciation.

I have decided that I will love myself when no one else does. I have decided to present myself to the world as a gorgeous, beautiful, and attractive woman as much as I possibly can. I do not need permission to be beautiful.

I have decided to look my best at all times. I am determined to take care of my body, my health, my spirit and my mind.

I refuse to sit around and let the doors of opportunity pass me by. I will try to absorb all the knowledge that my brain can possibly attain.

If necessary, I will drain the fountain of intelligence completely dry. It is true, knowledge is power, but we must be wise in how we use it.

Although beauty is important, I have decided that life is not about the fancy clothes, the fine cars, and the big house. Life is about loving self and others with an internal and eternal perspective.

I have decided that I will continue to make an effort to love and understand all people, no matter how difficult or how strange the circumstances maybe.

I have decided that I am going to continue living and doing the things that I truly believe. If others want to laugh and exert their simplicity, they have my permission.

I have decided that it is always important to know who I am, where I am, and what I am doing. Besides God, I am the CEO of my life and its situations.

I have decided that my happiness starts and ends with me. I no longer depend on others to make my heart merry. If I need a vacation, I take it.

I have decided that people come in all categories. Some I understand and some I do not. I have learned and I am still learning to appreciate and respect uniqueness.

As a nation, I hope that all people will find it important to love, respect, and value the gifts and talents that we have been granted.

It is my sincere hope that we will use our talents and gifts to create a world that is capable of attaining peace, fairness, hope and respect for all mankind.

At the End of the Day

At the end of the day, are you able to shut your eyes knowing that you have given your all to every situation or to someone who was placed in your path?

At the end of the day, do you feel that you have done what is right and fair without interrupting and destroying the welfare of another human's life?

At the end of the day, are you able to look back and count at least one seed that you have sown?

Are you able to recall one positive thing you said or did without uttering a complaint?

At the end of the day, are you able to walk with your head tall and body erect because you are not deliberating over some action or decision that you truly regret?

Are you able to say that you are proud of the woman you proclaim?

At the end of the day, are you able to say that you have lived well, or do you have to sit and recount the hidden acts that you are afraid to tell?

At the end of the day, when the sun has set, and you put your body down, are you a woman who is able to say deep within your heart that you lived each moment doing your very, very best?

It is a simple message, yet it is real. For each moment that we do not give our best, that is the very moment that we've cheated ourselves.

When we give our best, great things will eventually return. My sisters, this is a simple lesson. May we all listen and learn.

Relax

Sisters, it is time to relax. It is time to settle down. Pull your hair back and simply unwind.

You've had a long day. Work was no joke. The paperwork, the drama, lifting and squatting may have made it challenging to cope.

Stop! Do not look at the bills. No, it's not okay to swallow just one more stress pill.

Let go. Take your mind off the world. It is okay to experience self-appreciation.
It is a small gift for your hard work and unyielding dedication. Show yourself a little love.

Walk to the tub. Run the water. Let the bubbles swell. It's time to
toss the day away. Step in. You'll be okay.

Unwind your spirit as you softly say, it feels good to have this simple little get away.

It feels so sweet to go undisturbed. I can't believe I've allowed the pressures of the day to get me so perturbed.

As I recline, I give the beauty of this water the keys to unlock my mind.
I ask that it release all issues and concerns that are running faster than time.

I want this precious and most needed time to last. I'm going to enjoy the freedom of my bath, a new found path. It's my get away.

I am beginning to feel the peace that my body is bringing over me.

Why haven't I stopped to relax more often? As of this moment, the world will no longer make me holler. I will not let it make me scream.

I'll let this warm, bubbly water take me to the height of my fanciest dreams.

I am tired of being manipulated by what I think is success, when all I'm gaining is high blood pressure and stress.

I refuse to let the events of a day, a week, a month, or any time take my serenity away.
When all else fails, I know that I can always bow my head and pray.

I will relax in the midst of it all. My mind, my body, and spirit will engulf all the beauty and harmony my soul can take.

From now on, failing to relax will no longer be my mistake. I'll rest. I will not let hustle and bustle of the day deplete my sanity.

Session 8:

Keeping It Real

Self-Assessment 101

I, _____, promise to respond to all statements in an honorable manner. I will not lie. I will not cheat, and I will not straddle the fence when marking or thinking of my answers. The truth will be the truth.

In order to pass this test, you must answer all questions deeply from the heart.

- Whenever I stand before a mirror, I love and adore the image that stares me in the face.

- I make a conscious effort to look and feel beautiful everyday.

- I have at least two girlfriends who will stop whatever they are doing and come to my rescue at any given time.

- I have a strong and beautiful relationship with my mother and sister (s).

- I have set at least one powerful and life changing goal over the past year and accomplished it.

- I am not living in an abusive situation, whether it is physical, emotional, or mental.

- I make it a point to pursue knowledge through academic or personal endeavors (reading, self-help courses, community outreach programs, etc.) as much as I possibly can.

- I make an effort to treat my family, my friends, my neighbors, colleagues, etc., with respect and appreciation at all times.

- I make it a point to be totally honest with myself about who I am and the things I do when behind close doors.

- When I am discouraged, I am able to see something positive in my situation.

- I believe that my life means something, and I was placed on this earth for a special reason.

- I make it a priority to pursue truth and righteousness in all that I say and do.

- When others think less of me, criticize my potential, or doubt my reason for doing something, I am able to look beyond their negativity and see the power that lies within me.

- When my mind starts to turn on a negative axis, I know how to redirect my thoughts and get back on a positive rotation.

- When I know that I am wrong or have wronged someone, I am humble enough and woman enough to admit my mistakes and apologize as needed, if needed.

- I am woman enough to stay away from the socially disfiguring disease called gossip that hurts and destroys the soul, reputation, and character of my family, friends, co-workers, etc.

- What was your outcome? Record it in your mind. Use your responses as a tool for self-empowerment. May your life take you beyond your wildest dreams!

Session 9:

Positive Thoughts for the Soul

If you desire, you may practice saying these affirmations to yourself on a daily basis. They are very encouraging and good for the soul. You'd be amazed at the impact they can have on the mind, body, soul and spirit.

I am a very smart woman.

I am a very beautiful woman.

I am a very positive woman.

I feel good about myself.

I truly love myself.

I am looking forward to becoming a better woman as each day goes by.

I am an achiever.

I will reach my goals.

I am very loving.

I am kind to others.

I am a woman of a quiet and gentle spirit.

I love to laugh and have fun.

I am special.

I am a great mother, wife, sister, friend and co-worker.

I expect great things to occur in my life on a daily basis.

I am a winner.

I love and appreciate the QUEEN that is within my soul.

I am beautiful. I am smart, and I am love.

Session 10:

Words for the Soul

On those days when life just feels blah, take God's word directly to your heart and soul. May they bathe and refresh the girl, the woman, the wife, the sister, the neighbor, and the friend within you. In other words, may they bring you back to life, so that you maybe life to others.

To my sisters, when you are down and out and feel that life has been over-whelming and unbearable, you may refer, if you desire to the passages below as a source of encouragement. If you do not believe in God, it is okay to practice the art of positive thinking and positive living. Repeat positive affirmations about yourself to yourself repeatedly.

Psalms 18:1, 4, 6, 16, and 18 (NLT)

I love you Lord. You are my strength. The Lord is my rock, my protection, and my savior.

I can run to him for safety. He is my shield, my saving strength, and my tower. I will call to the Lord.

The ropes of death bound me. The deadly rivers overwhelmed me. The ropes of death were before me.

In my trouble I called to the Lord. I cried to my God for help. From his temple He heard my voice. My call for help reached his ears.

The Lord reached down from above and took me. He pulled me from the deep water.

Those who hated me were too strong for me, but the Lord supported me. He took me to a safe place.

Philippians 4:13 (NKJV)
I can do all things through Christ who strengthens me.

Psalms 32:4-5 (NIV)

When I kept silent, my bones wasted away through my groaning all day long. For day and night, your hand was heavy upon me. My strength was sapped as in the heat of summer. Then I acknowledged my sin (heart, fears, my secrets, etc.) to you and did not cover up my iniquity. I said, "I will confess my transgressions to the Lord" and you forgave the guilt of my sin.

II Corinthians 4:8-9 (NIV)

We are hard pressed on every side, but not crushed; perplexed, but not in despair; persecuted, but not abandoned; struck down, but not destroyed.

Romans 12:18 (NIV)

If it is possible, as far as it depends on you, live at peace with everyone.

Psalms 139: 1-3 (ESV)

O Lord, you have searched me and you know me. You know when I sit and when I rise; you perceive my thoughts from afar. You discern my lying down; you are familiar with all of my ways...

Isaiah 43:1-3 (ESV)

Fear not, for I have redeemed you; I have called you by name; you are mine. When you pass through the waters I will be with you; and when you pass through the rivers, they will not sweep over you; when you walk through the fire, you will not be burned; the flames will not set you ablaze. For I am the Lord, your God, the Holy One of Israel, your Savior.

Psalms 27:5-6 (NIV)

For on the day of trouble he will keep me safe in his dwelling; he will hide me in the shelter of his tabernacle and set me high on a rock. Then my head will be exalted above my enemies who surround me; at his tabernacle I will sacrifice with shouts of joy; I will sing and make music to the Lord.

Psalms 62: 5-8 (NIV)

Find rest, O my soul, in God alone; my hope comes from him. He alone is my rock and my salvation. He is my salvation, and my honor depend on God. He is my rock and my refuge.

I Thessalonians 4:17 (NIV)

Make it your ambition to live a quiet life, to mind your own business and to work with your hands just as we told you.

Jeremiah 29:11 (NIV)

For I know the plans I have for you, declares the Lord, plans to prosper you and not harm you, plans to give you hope and a future...

Exodus 33:17 (NIV)

And God said to Moses, "I will do the very thing you have asked me, because I know you by name."

Genesis 12:12 (NIV)

I will make you a great nation, and I will bless you and make your name great, so that you will be a blessing.

Psalms 18: 1-3 (NIV)

God is my rock, my fortress, my deliverer, my shield, my stronghold. I will call upon the Lord, who is worthy to be praised, and so shall I be saved from my enemies.

Deuteronomy 31:6 (NIV)

Be strong and courageous. Do not be afraid or terrified because of them, for the Lord your God goes with you. He will never leave you not forsake you.

Exodus 14:14 (ESV)

The Lord will fight for you, you just stay silent.

Psalms 27:1 (KJV)

The Lord is my light and my salvation; whom shall I fear? The Lord is the strength of my life; of whom shall I be afraid?

Luke 1:37 (KJV)

For nothing will be impossible with God.

Job 42:2 (NIV)

I know that you can do everything and that no purpose of yours can be withheld from you.

John 3:20 (ESV)

God is greater than our worried hearts and knows more about us than we do about ourselves.

John 16:24 (ESV)

Until now you have not asked for anything in my name. Ask and you will receive, and your joy will be complete.

Hebrews 13:5 (NLT)

"Don't love money; be satisfied with what you have. For God said, "I will never leave you. I will never forsake you. I will never abandon you."

Session 11:

Words to Ponder- No Blunders- They Say What They Say

Women, allow your beautiful hearts, your love, your kindness and your integrity to resonate in all aspects of life.

Make an effort to maintain a quiet and gentle spirit. You will be heard and noticed much sooner.

Do not tell everything you know. The person you trust most will be the first to tell.

Express your words carefully. Careless words can be very painful to another person's soul.

Do not believe everything you hear. Think about the message. Analyze the messenger.

Do not lose your temper. Remain calm. Anger shows a form of weakness.

Pursue as much knowledge as you can. Remain a lifelong learner. Study many ideas. Read many books.

Always think before you give an answer.

Speak pleasant words. You will win people over. People laugh at our stupidity but embrace our intelligence.

Never make fun of the poor. If you do, you are insulting yourself, the individual, his or her parents and God.

Always listen to both sides of the story.

Before approaching the ring, study your opponent carefully.

Be open to listening to the ideas and advice of others, but within your mind, know that God is the one who holds the answers. That is my opinion and my belief.

If you are careful about what you say, you will keep yourself out of a lot of trouble.

Be careful as to how you conduct yourself in front of others. Someone is always watching what you say and what you do and will turn and use it against you.

If you see danger, avoid it. Do not walk into the trap.

Always listen to your parent(s) advice.

The least we can do is search for the truth in any matter that pertains to our lives.

Keep your mind on what is right.

Avoid arrogance. Practice humility. Humility is power.

Do not sleep too long. You don't want to become lazy and poor. Work smart for the things you deserve.

If someone wants to argue and fight, use gentle words. Your voice will be heard. Allow that individual the honor of destructing him or herself. Reputation is powerful!

Take a journey inside your mind to see what you can find.

Always know the status of your condition. Pay attention to what is going on in your life.

Practice peace daily. It will keep you calm and make you sleep well at night.

Live one life. Keep it clean. Untruths will be exposed.

If you've been warned once, take heed. If you've been warned twice, take heed. The third time you may be hurt beyond cure. Don't turn a dull ear to your intuition.

Always speak up for the poor and the needy. Treat them fairly.

Always love and respect yourself. Do the same for others.

Tell God exactly what you want. Do not beat around the bush.

If you want money, start saving in small increments. You'd be amazed at how pennies grow.

If you want to become a powerful woman, put a book in your hand. As your brain discovers new ideas, they may return a profit in some shape, form, or fashion.

If you do nothing else in life, get up and try to accomplish something. You can accomplish anything you desire by exercising intelligence and putting forth effort on a consistent basis.

Session 12:

Epilogue

Wow! How do you feel? I hope that you feel convicted, inspired, appreciated, triumphant, amazed, and encouraged. I hope that as you embarked upon your journey, you came across pieces of writing that left you with the idea that you are an incredible woman who deserves the best of everything. I hope that you were able to find your soul, your life, and your experiences somewhere in this book of poetic perspectives.

I hope that you have discovered a tool of encouragement that can be used daily or as often as needed. I believe that the writings will lift your spirit and energy in a positive direction. I hope that you never put this book aside. I believe that it was inspired by God as a tool to give ALL women hope and inspiration.

As you analyzed the content of this book, I hope that you were able to discover that there is no reason to live life on this earth as an individual who is sad, lonely, depressed and without hope. I'm learning to embrace the belief that God wants no man or woman to be void of life's outstanding opportunities.

May we all walk away from this book as empowered women. However, that decision is personal. May it cause us to take action and make needed decisions to live our most empowered lives, if we so desire. That decision is personal.

Sisters, I wish you all the success you need and then some. May God grant you the tools needed to be an incredible human being as you continue your existence upon the face of this earth. I will say it again, "You were created to be a powerful and successful woman." Let not life's circumstances rob you of your opportunity to be bold, happy, beautiful and free.

As you open your eyes each morning, realize that you have been afforded an opportunity to experience life at least one more day. Do not take your existence for granted. Make it your business to live each moment as if you are proud to be alive. Laugh, have fun and reach your goals.

You have the right to live. Approval is granted each day as you are able to step foot out of bed. At some appointed time, this moment will cease to exist. Therefore, strive abundantly and expectantly to live life to the best of your ability.

Beautifully,

Dr. Mary E. Robinson

Session 13:

About the Author

"Doc Robie"

Dr. Mary E. Robinson was born in Alabama. She spent most of her summers as a child and teenager in North Chicago, Illinois. It was during those years that she was truly exposed to cultural diversity on every level.

Dr. Robinson is a two-time graduate of Alabama A. & M. University where she completed her Bachelor's in Social Work and Master's in Education. She completed her Specialist's Degree in Educational Leadership Administration and Supervision at Cambridge College in Cambridge, Massachusetts. She completed her Doctorate in Educational Leadership from Argosy University. She completed an L-5 in Educational Leadership Administration and Supervision from the State University of West Georgia at Carrollton, and she completed an ESOL Endorsement aimed at supporting English Language Learners in the areas of reading and math.

During her professional tenure, she was nominated as Who's Who Among America's Teachers. She was nominated as Teacher of Year in the DeKalb County School District in Georgia. She was recognized as an ALL STAR TEACHER in 2009 via Parent Recognition. In 1995, she received Superintendent Recognition via the Clayton County School District in Jonesboro, Georgia, and she received personal recognition/letter via a Musical Performance at Lake Ridge Elementary School's Dedication Ceremony from a member of the House of Representative.

Dr. Robinson has worked as an educator for the past 24 years. She loves God's word. She enjoys antiquing, traveling, live music, singing, drumming, writing, reading, eating great food, radio hosting, and studying historical events.

Printed in the United States
By Bookmasters